STORYFUN
1

STUDENT'S BOOK

with Online Activities
and Home Fun Booklet 1

Karen Saxby

Cambridge University Press
www.cambridge.org/elt

Cambridge Assessment English
www.cambridgeenglish.org

Information on this title: www.cambridge.org/9781316617014

© Cambridge University Press 2017

First published 2011
Second edition 2017

30 29 28 27 26 25

Printed in Malaysia by Vivar Printing

A catalogue record for this publication is available from the British Library

ISBN 978-1-316-61701-4 Student's Book with online activities and Home Fun booklet
ISBN 978-1-316-61706-9 Teacher's Book with Audio
ISBN 978-1-316-61712-0 Presentation Plus

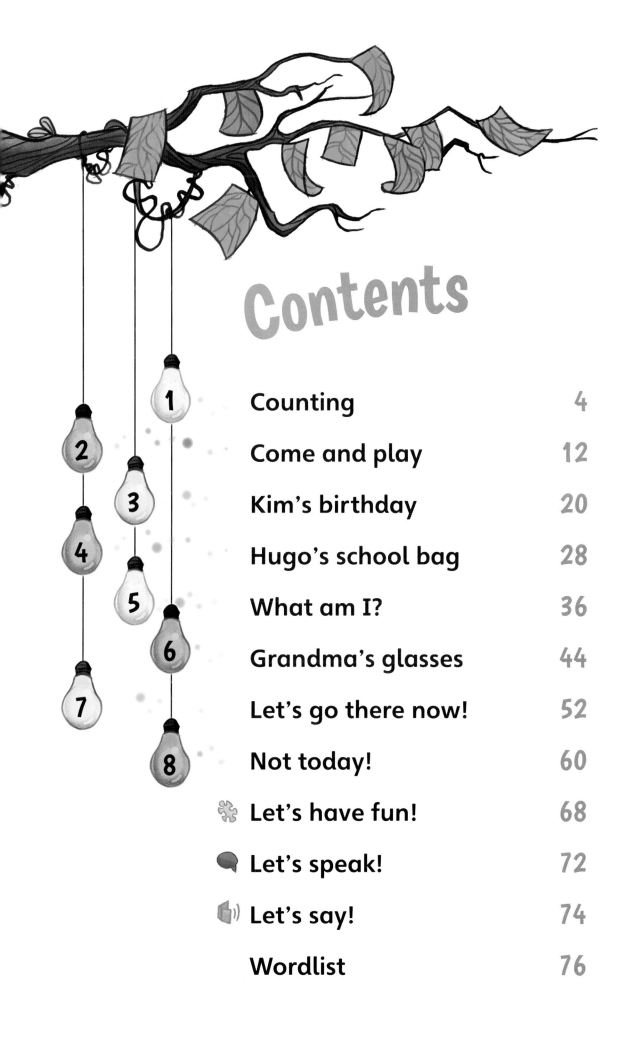

Contents

Counting

Hi! My name's Ben and I'm your friend.

And this is Sam. Sam is my dog.

Sam plays with my shoes. Sam? My shoes, please!

My name's Ben and I'm your friend.

1, 2, 3 Count with me!

4, 5, 6, 7 Silly Sam! My blue shoe, please!

Good dog, Sam. Well done!
Right! 8, 9, 10.
Let's count again.

1, 2, 3 That's right! With me!

4, 5, 6, 7 and 8.

That's really, really, really great!

Oh, and then,
It's 9 and ...?
Silly Sam.
My red boot, please!

Good dog, Sam.

Well done!

So ... How many?
It's 9 and 10.
Goodbye!

Counting

A Draw lines.

a  b  c  d

❶ blue ❷ dog ❸ red ❹ shoe

B Draw, count and write.

1   2   4   5   6   8   10

C Read, draw and write.

Hi! My name's Eva.

Hi! My name's Dan.

Hi! My name's
....

D ▶ **03** Listen. Ask and answer.

We're Ben's friends!

He's a boy.

She's a girl.

What's your name?

EVA

DAN

E ▶ **Listen and write numbers.**
04

F **Draw lines and say.**

1

a Goodbye! Goodbye!

2

b Well done, Sam! Well done!

3

c Silly Sam! My red ball, please!

▶ Listen and tick (✔) the box.
05

1

☐   ✔

2

☐    ☐

3

☐   ☐

H Read and draw.

1 girl

1 dog

2 boys

3 phones

p. 68

p. 72

11

Come and play

Hi! I'm Anna.
I've got two cars
and four guitars!

Come and play
with me today!

I've got three kites
and a yellow bike.
Come and play
with me today!

Hi! I'm Tom.

I've got some bats
and some funny red hats!

Come and play
with me today!

I've got five ducks
and two big trucks.
Come and play
with me today!

My name's Sue.
I've got a doll.
And look!
Here's my blue book!

My name's Pat.
I've got a lizard
and lots of pears
and here's my
happy teddy bear.
Come and play
with us today!

We've got lots of pets, too.

They can play with you!

We've got a cat, a dog and three green frogs.

So clap your hands and come and play.

Come and play with us today!

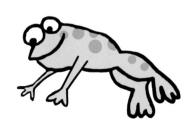

2

Come and play

A Draw lines.

ⓐ

ⓒ

❶ duck

❷ frog

❸ kite

ⓑ

ⓓ

❹ pear

B Look, read and write the names.

Anna̶ Pat Sue Tom

Hello! I'm
.....Anna....... .

My name's
....

I'm ....

Hi! My name's
....

C Put a tick (✔) or a cross (✘) in the box.

1 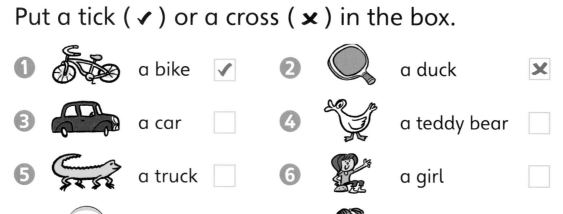 a bike ✔   2 a duck ✘

3 a car ☐   4 a teddy bear ☐

5 a truck ☐   6 a girl ☐

7 a ball ☐   8 a pear ☐

D Look and write.

The robots have got one **1** b _a g_ , one **2** b _ _ _ , one
3 g _ _ _ _ _ and one **4** d _ _ _ .
The robots have got two **5** h _ _ _ , two **6** k _ _ _ _ and two
7 b _ _ _ .
The robots have got three **8** d _ _ _ _ , four **9** p _ _ _ _ _ _ and
five **10** b _ _ _ _ , too!

E Look and say.

> They've got four hats!

F Look and read. Write *yes* or *no*.

1 Pat has got a cat. ....yes........

2 The cat has got a truck. ....no.........

3 Sue has got a red pencil. ....

4 The children have got seven bats. ....

5 The big robot has got four pencils. ....

6 Tom has got two books. ....

7 Anna has got six trucks. ....

▶ Listen and colour.
07

G Write and draw.

1. Here's my .....mouse....... .
2. Here's my ....
3. Here's my ....
4. Here's my ....
5. Here's my ....

H Say the words. Draw lines.

bat   cat   dog   duck   hat

truck

frog

Pat

p. 68

p. 72

Kim's birthday

It's my birthday today!

Hooray! Hooray!

This is my mum and dad.

This is my brother, Dan.

This is my sister.

Her name's Jill!

And Grandpa's here, too!

My grandpa's name is Bill.

I love him!

It's my birthday today! Hooray! Hooray!

I've got lots of cards and a new box of paints.

These are my presents, too! Look!

Is this a bat?
No, it's a
sun hat.

Is this a clock?
No, they're
some socks.

Is this a toy tiger?
No, it's a
toy spider!

It's my birthday today! Hooray! Hooray!
It's my party now. We've got lemonade and ice cream!
But where's my toy spider? It's on Grandpa's head!

This cake is great!
And now I'm eight!
How old are you?
Are you eight, too?

Thank you, Mum and Dad and Jill.
And thank you, Dan and Grandpa Bill!

3

Kim's birthday

A Draw lines.

ⓐ   ⓑ   ⓒ   ⓓ

❶ clock   ❷ ice cream   ❸ **paints**   ❹ **spider**

B Look, read and write.

brother   dad   grandpa   ~~mum~~   sister

This is me!
My name's Kim.

❸  This is my ....

❶  This is my ...*mum*............ .

❹  This is my ....

❷  This is my ....

❺  And look! This is my

....

C Which are Kim's presents? Put a tick (✔) or a cross (✘) in the box.

☐ ☐ ☐ ☐ ☐ ☐

D Read and choose a word. Write.

balloons cake hats lemonade ~~party~~ songs

1

Let's have a ...party......... .

2

Let's make some party ....

3

Let's make a big ....

4

Let's sing lots of ....

5

Let's get some ....

6

Let's have some ....

E Look and read. Write *yes* or *no*.

1. Kim's sun hat is yellow. ....yes........
2. Kim's sister has got a hat. ....no........
3. Kim's brother is in the picture. ....
4. The balloons are red and blue. ....
5. Kim has got some lemonade. ....
6. The kite is pink and blue. ....

F ▶ Listen and colour.
09

G Draw lines.

1. Is this a bat?
2. Happy birthday!
3. Where's my toy spider?
4. How old are you?
5. Let's play some games!

a. I'm seven!
b. OK! Great!
c. It's under the chair.
d. Thank you!
e. No, it's a sun hat!

H Draw your present for Kim.

Thank you!

I Listen and sing the song.

10

* It's my birthday today! Hooray! Hooray!
* It's a happy, happy, happy, happy day.

Mum and **1** .... are here. And Jill!
My brother Dan and Grandpa Bill.

We've got lemonade and chocolate **2** ....
And now I'm not seven. Now I'm **3** .... !

Thank you, Mum and Dad and Jill.
And thank you, Dan and Grandpa Bill.

p. 69

p. 72

27

Hugo's school bag

It's a school day today! Right! What's in my bag?

My new crayons and paints. My old eraser and phone.

But where is my ruler? Oh! There, with my book.

And where is my pen? Oh! There it is. Good!

Look at the clock! Bye, Mum. Bye, Sue.

I've got my school bag. See you!

Run to the bus stop. Quick! Quick!

And jump on the bus. Hi, Grace! Hello, Nick!

We love our new playground.
Let's have some fun.
Here! Catch this ball.
And jump and run!

This is my classroom.
And this is Miss Rice.
She's our new teacher.
She's really nice.

We're making a poster.
Right! What's in my bag?
My new crayons and paints.
My old eraser and phone.

But where is my ruler?
It's not here with my book.
And where is my pen?
It's not here. Oh no! Look!

'Don't worry!' says Mark.

Here you are!

Have my ruler.
I've got two!
They're for you.'

'It's OK!' says May.
'Here you are! Have my pen.
I've got three!
For you and me!'

Thank you!
Thank you!

4 Hugo's school bag

A Draw lines.

a
b
c
d
e
f

1 This is my **pen**!

2 Here's my **school bag**.

3 This is my teacher.

4 Here are my crayons.

5 This is my **ruler**.

6 And here's the **bus**!

B Look, read and write.

1 Hugo has a sister.   Her name is **S u e**

2 Hugo has a new teacher.   Her name is **Miss R _ c _** .

3 Hugo sees a girl on the bus.   Her name is **G _ a _ e**.

4 Hugo sees a boy on the bus.   His name is **_ i c _** .

5 A boy gives Hugo a ruler.   His name is **M _ r k**.

6 A girl gives Hugo a pen.   Her name is **_ a _** .

C Ask and answer.
Look and point.

Where's the ball?

Here it is.
Where are the birds?

D Listen and say.

12

A B C D E F G H I J K L M
N O P Q R S T U V W X Y Z

E Choose and draw a blue line from the ruler to the pen.
Ask and answer and draw a red line.

A, J, ...

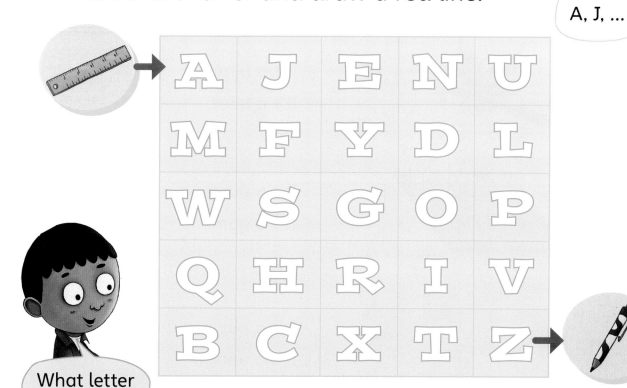

What letter isn't here?

F ▶ Listen and draw lines.

13

Alex   Eva   May

Mark   Lucy

G Read and choose the correct answer.

1

It's a classroom.

(It's a computer.) ✗

2

It's a bird.

It's a boot.

3

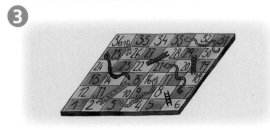

It's a name.

It's a game.

4

It's a playground.

It's a pencil.

H Write. Ask and answer.

What's in your school bag?

I've got ...

My school bag
....
....
....
....

My friend's school bag
....
....
....
....

I ▶ Listen and sing the song.
14

My **1** .... is so cool.

My lessons are great.

How **2** .... are

my classmates?

We're seven and eight!

My teacher's so **3** ....

Her name is Miss File.

She's got lots of **4** ....

and a really big smile!

Yes, our school's really **5** ....

Our lessons are GREAT!

6 .... , our school's really cool.

Our lessons are GREAT!

p. 69

p. 72

What am I?

Excuse me!
What am I?
Can you tell me, please?

Well, you aren't an elephant.
I'm an elephant and my body is very big.
Your body is very small.
Have you got big ears?

No, I haven't.

Well, elephants have got big ears.
No. You aren't an elephant. Sorry!

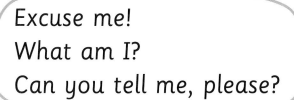

Excuse me!
What am I?
Can you tell me, please?

Well, you aren't a crocodile.
I'm a crocodile and I've got lots of long white, teeth.
You haven't got teeth.
Have you got a long tail?

No, I haven't.
My tail is short.

Well, crocodiles have got long tails.
No. You aren't a crocodile.
Sorry!

Excuse me!
What am I?
Please tell me!

Well, you aren't a monkey.
I'm a monkey and I've got a funny face
You haven't got a funny face!
Can you climb trees?

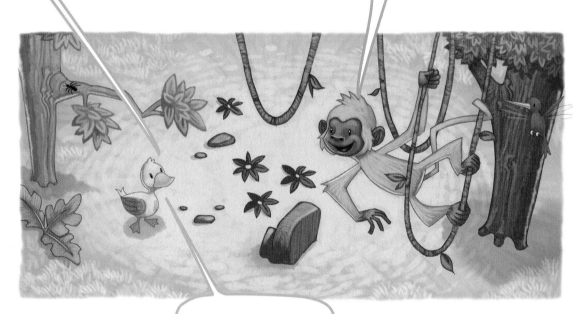

No, I can't!

Well, monkeys
can climb trees.
No. You aren't a monkey.
Sorry!

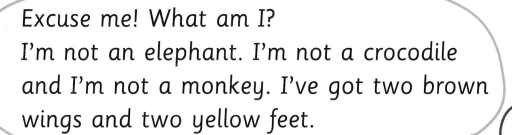

Excuse me! What am I?
I'm not an elephant. I'm not a crocodile and I'm not a monkey. I've got two brown wings and two yellow feet.

Me too!

I can swim.
I can walk and I can fly.

Me too!
You're a duck, you see!
You're a duck like me!

I'm a **DUCK!**
Yippee!

What am I?

A Draw lines.

ⓐ   ⓑ   ⓒ   ⓓ

❶ **crocodile**   ❷ **duck**   ❸ **elephant**   ❹ **monkey**

B Which animals does the duck talk to? Choose and colour the path yellow.

C Who is correct? Read and write.

The duck says, 'No, I'm not a duck. Sorry! I can't swim, walk or fly.'

Eva

The duck says, 'Please tell me.' It wants answers to lots of questions.

Sam

The duck can't understand the elephant, crocodile or the monkey.

Lucy

.... is correct!

D Look at the pictures. Look at the letters. Write the words.

 1

This is an _eye_.

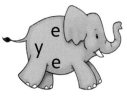
e
y
e

 2

This is an _ _ _ .

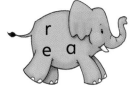
r
e a

 **3**

This is a _ _ _ .

g
e l

 4

This is a _ _ _ _ .

d y
b o

 5

This is a _ _ _ _ .

o t
f o

 **6**

This is a _ _ _ _ _ .

t m
h o u

E Read and choose the crocodile's answer.

1 Can you fly? Yes, I can. / (No, I can't.)

2 Can you swim? Yes, I can. / No, I can't.

3 Can you walk? Yes, I can. / No, I can't.

4 Can you jump? Yes, I can. / No, I can't.

F 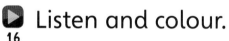 Listen and colour.

16

How many monkeys are there in the picture? ....

G Read and choose the correct answer.

1. Monkeys love **burgers** / (**bananas**) / **fish**.
2. Monkeys have got long **arms** / **noses** / **feet**.
3. Hippos can **sing** / **climb** / **swim**.
4. Monkeys have got two **wings** / **hands** / **tails**.
5. Elephants can **talk** / **jump** / **walk**.
6. Spiders can **run** / **fly** / **count**.

H Look, read and write.

1. What are you?   *a crocodile and an elephant.*
2. What colour is your body? .... and ....
3. What colour are your eyes? ....
4. Have you got a long tail? ....
5. Can you talk?   ....
6. Can you fly?   ....

I Read the questions. Ask and answer.

Are you a boy or a girl?

What colour are your eyes?

Have you got long hair?

Can you swim?

p. 70

p. 73

Grandma's glasses

Grandma is at Jill's house.
She wants to go home now,
but she can't find her glasses.
'I've got my handbag and I've
got my coat.
I've got my toothbrush and
I've got my bike.
But where are my glasses?'
asks Grandma.

I can help!

Let's look on the table and in
the cupboard, too!' says Tom.
'No! Your glasses aren't here!
But look! Wow! My robot!
Great!'

'Let's look under the TV and next to the computer,' says Jill. 'No! They aren't here! But look! Wow! My old ruler! Great!'

'Let's look next to the armchairs and under the cushions,' says Mum. 'No! Your glasses aren't here! But look! Wow! My red socks! Great!'

'Oh dear! With no glasses, I can't ride
my bike!' Grandma says.
'We can drive you home!' Dad says.

'Can we come too?' ask Tom and Jill.
'Yes, you can!' says Dad.

'Thank you,' says Grandma.
'Wow! It's hot in here!'
'Grandma!' Tom and Jill say,
'Your glasses are on your head!'

'Fantastic!' says Grandma.
'Now I can ride home.'

6

Grandma's glasses

A Draw lines.

① car **②** computer **③** glasses

 a  b  c  d  e

④ handbag **⑤** home

B Look and read the questions. Write one-word answers.

① What can't Grandma find?   her ....

② What is the boy's name?   ....

③ What does Jill find?   her ....

④ Who finds some socks?   ....

⑤ Where are Grandma's glasses?   on her ....

⑥ What can Grandma ride?   a ....

C Write a, b or c in the boxes.

a Tom **b** Jill **c** Mum

 1  2 3

 4  5  6

48

D Draw lines.

a TV

a rug

a desk

an armchair

a table

a clock

a cupboard

a sofa

Look and read the questions. Write one-word answers.

1 What colour is the armchair? ......orange......

2 What colour is the table? ....

3 What colour is the sofa? ....

4 What colour is the cupboard? ....

E Read and choose the correct answer.

~~in~~ next to on on under under

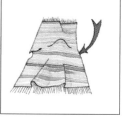

The cat's looking **1** ....in......... the cupboard and **2** ....
the sofa and **3** .... the table and **4** .... the TV
and **5** .... the desk and **6** .... the rug!

F Look at the pictures. Look at the letters.
Write and colour.

1 This is Grandma's blue ....*hat*........ .

a t
h

2 This is Jill's pink ....

u r
e l
r

3 This is Tom's black ....

t
b o
r o

4 These are Mum's red ....

s s
o k
c

5 These are Grandma's purple ....

s
e s
s l
a g

G Look, read and write the number.

1 How many people can you see? ....5..........

2 How many animals can you see? ....

3 How many flowers can you see? ....

4 How many children can you see? ....

H Listen and colour.
18

 I Draw the things in your room. Then talk and point.

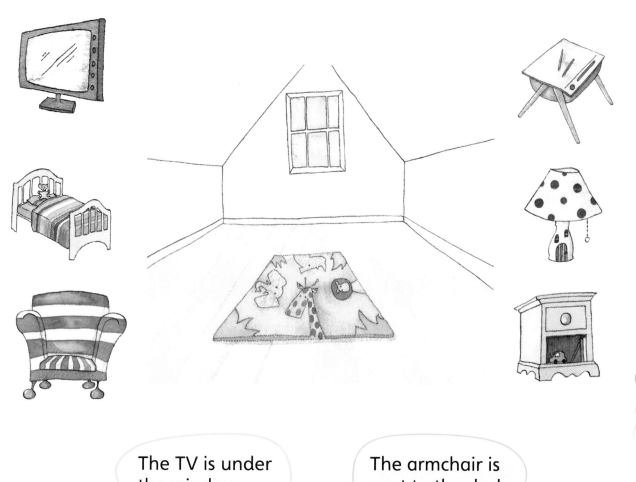

The TV is under the window.

The armchair is next to the desk.

p. 70

p. 73

7 Let's go there now!

Matt and Alice live next to the beach in Sea Street.

In the morning, Matt sees Alice at the bus stop. Matt and Alice like lots of sports.

'Hi, Alice!' Matt says. 'I've got badminton today. I love badminton. Do you?'
'No,' Alice answers. 'But I really like horse riding!'
'I don't,' says Matt.
'Bye! See you!'

At lunchtime, Alice sees Matt at the sports shop.

'Hi again, Matt!' Alice says. 'I love tennis. Do you?'

'Tennis? No! But baseball is a great sport!' says Matt.

says Alice. 'Bye! See you!'

In the afternoon, Matt sees Alice in the playground. 'Hello again!' Matt says. 'I love skateboarding! Do you?' 'Yes, I do!' says Alice. 'Which is your skateboard, Matt?' 'The red one,' answers Matt. 'And which is your skateboard, Alice?' 'The grey one,' Alice answers. 'Where do you go skateboarding?' 'In the park!' says Matt. 'Me too!' says Alice.

'Let's go and skateboard there!' says Matt.
'OK,' says Alice. 'Yes! Let's go there now!'

'My father and I like fishing here, too. Do you?' asks Alice.

'No, I don't,' answers Matt. 'I don't like fishing!'

'Do you like swimming, Matt?' asks Alice.

'Yes, I do!' says Matt!

7

Let's go there now!

A Draw lines.

① badminton **②** baseball **③** fishing

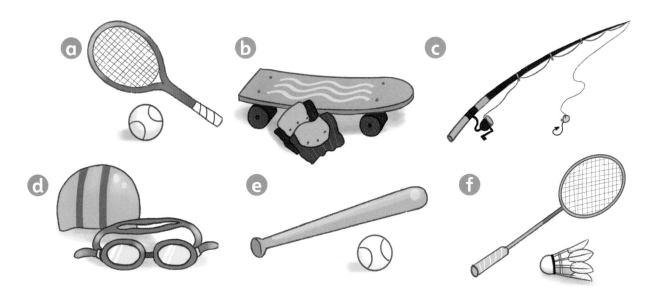

④ skateboarding **⑤** swimming **⑥** tennis

B Read and put a tick (✔) in the boxes.

	Matt	Alice
1 Who likes horse riding?	☐	✔
2 Who likes tennis?	☐	☐
3 Who loves badminton?	☐	☐
4 Who loves fishing?	☐	☐
5 Who loves baseball?	☐	☐
6 Who loves skateboarding?	☐	☐

C Where's Matt? Look, read and write the number.

1 He's at the playground!

2 He's at the beach! He loves swimming.

3 He's at home. Look!

4 He's at the park! He loves the park.

5 He's there! At the sports shop.

6 Look! He's at the bus stop.

 D ▶ Listen and draw lines.
20

E Read and put a tick (✔) in the box.

	🙂	🙁
baseball		
tennis		
swimming		
football		
fishing		
horse riding		
badminton		
skateboarding		

Now ask and answer.

Do you like tennis?   Yes, I do.

Do you like swimming?   No, I don't.

F ▶ Listen and write a name or a number.
21

1 What is this girl's name?   ....Kim........

2 How old is she?   ....8..........

3 Where is her school?   next to
.... Park

4 Who is her favourite friend?   ....

5 How many tennis balls has she got?   ....

6 What is her tennis teacher's name?   Mrs ....

7 How many sports shoes has she got?   ....

58

G Read, draw and colour.

Alice loves tennis.

She's got her tennis racket but she hasn't got her tennis ball.

She's got a yellow tennis ball and purple tennis shoes in her sports bag.

Matt likes baseball.

He's got his baseball but he hasn't got his bat!

He's got a grey baseball bat and an orange baseball cap in his sports bag.

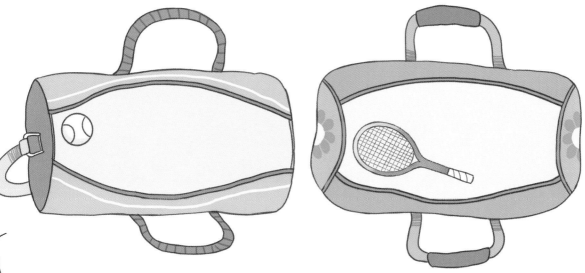

H Look, read and write.

At the park you can ...

....

....

....

....

p. 71

p. 73

8

Not today!

Dan and his sister, Lucy, are with their mother in Mr Chip's food shop.

Can we have some oranges or some nice red grapes, Mum?

Not today, Dan. We've got a lot of fruit at home.

I love apple pie, Mum!

Me too! But no apple pie today

Dan and Lucy are at their favourite pet shop.

Not today!

A Draw lines.

❶ apple pie　　**❷ chickens**　　**❸ donkey**

❹ fish　　**❺ meatballs**

B Who wants this/these? Write, ask and answer.

Dan　　　Lucy　　　Mum

❶ .... ❷ .... ❸ .... ❹ ....

❺ .... ❻ .... ❼ .... ❽ ....

Who likes tomatoes?　　Dan!

C Read and choose the correct answer.

1. 'I'd like some oranges (**and**) / **but** some apple pie, please, Mr Chips!' asks Dan.

2. 'Can I have some tomatoes **and** / **but** a watch?' asks Lucy.

3. Dan wants some jeans **and** / **but** he doesn't want a new school shirt.

4. Mum doesn't want a chicken **and** / **but** she wants a donkey.

5. 'What do donkeys like eating?' Lucy asks.
'Carrots **and** / **but** fruit!' Dan answers.

D Look and read. Write *yes* or *no*.

1. Lucy's chair is yellow. ....yes........
2. Dan is eating an egg. ....no.........
3. You can see a computer. ....
4. The grapes are blue. ....
5. The glasses are under the book. ....
6. Dan is eating fish and chips. ....
7. There are five pears. ....
8. Lucy is eating a kiwi. ....

▶ Listen and tick (✔) the box.
23

①	a monkey	☐	a donkey	✔
②	a fish	☐	an elephant	☐
③	a snake	☐	a cat	☐
④	a spider	☐	a frog	☐
⑤	a crocodile	☐	a chicken	☐
⑥	a dog	☐	a hippo	☐

F **Read and choose a word. Write.**

watertailapplescrocodile(garden)

I live in Dan's ① .....garden...... .

I've got four legs and a long ② ....
but I'm not an elephant or a ③ ....

I'm a donkey! I don't drink lemonade but I
drink a lot of ④ ....

I love carrots, pears and ⑤ ....
Do you?

G **▶ Listen and draw lines.**
24

Alex   Bill   Pat

Nick   Sam

Listen and sing the song.

25

Six blue cakes!

And two long snakes!

Where are the cakes?

Oh no! Oh no!

Sorry!

Nine nice burgers

And three hungry tigers

Where are the burgers?

Oh no! Oh no!

Sorry!

Lots of white rice!

And five little mice!

Where is the rice?

Oh no! Oh no!

Sorry!

Eight big kiwis!

And four hungry monkeys!

Where are the kiwis?

Oh no! Oh no!

Sorry!

Ten lemon sweets!

For my friends and me to eat!

Where are all the sweets?

Yum! Yum! Yum!

p. 71

p. 73

Let's have fun!

1 Count and tick (✔). How many?

Look! That's red.

Look! That's blue.

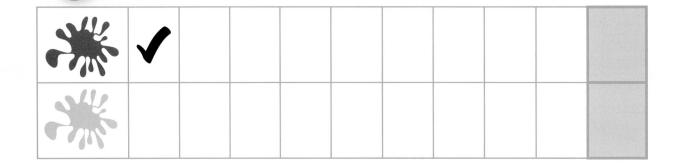	✔								

2 Make a poster.

I've got ...

a bike

a hat

a doll

a cat

3 Make a birthday card.

Happy Birthday! from

_____

4 Play a game. Bingo!

5 Play an animal game.

.........elephant.........

6 Make a picture and write.

yellow lamp

red sofa

brown table

7 Make a sports poster.

Football

shorts

T-shirt

park

8 Make a donkey.

carrot

Let's speak

1 How many? Play a game.

Two and two. Yes!

Well done!

2 Come and play with me today! Ask and answer.

Are you a doll?

No / Yes!

Come and play with me today!

3 What is it? Play a game.

Is it a dog?

No.

Is it a frog?

Yes. Well done!

4 What's your name? Ask and answer.

Can you spell your name?

T-O-M

5 Who is it? Play a game.

6 Where is it? Ask and answer. Colour.

7 What do you like? Ask and answer.

8 What's on the list? Play a game.

Let's say!

i
tennis

a
hand

e
bed

u
duck

o
dog

oo
book

p
piano

b
banana

d
doll

t
teddy bear

k/c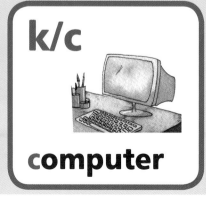
computer

g
green

l
lemonade

r
robot

m
monkey

n
nose

y
yellow

w
white

f
frog

v
li**v**ing room

s
sun

sh
shell

Wordlist

1 Counting

nouns

ball

boot

boy

dog

friend

girl

name

number

phone

right

shoe

adjectives

blue

good

great

red

right

silly

verbs

count

let's

play

expressions

goodbye

hi

how many

please

well done

2 Come and play

nouns

bat

bike

book

car

cat

dog

doll

duck

frog

guitar

hands

hat

kite

lizard

mouse

pear

pencil

pet

robot

table

teddy bear

today

truck

adjectives

big

blue

funny

green

happy

red

yellow

verbs

can

clap

colour

come

have got

3 Kim's birthday

nouns

balloon

box

brother

cake

card

chair

chocolate

clock

dad

day

fun

games

grandpa

head

ice cream

lemonade

mum

paints

party

picture

present

sister

sock

song

spider

sun

tiger

toy

adjectives

brown

new

old

pink

purple

verbs

get

have

look

love

make

sing

expressions

thank you

4 Hugo's school bag

nouns

bag

baseball cap

bird

bus stop

classmate

classroom

computer

lesson

pen

pencil

playground

poster

ruler

school

smile

adjectives

cool

nice

quick

verbs

give

jump

run

say

see

prepositions

in

on

under

expressions

bye

don't worry

5 What am I?

nouns

answer

arm

banana

body

burger

colour

crocodile

ear

elephant

eye

face

feet/foot

flower

hair

hippo

leg

monkey

mouth

nose

question

tail

teeth

tree

water

wing

adjectives

long

short

white

verbs

climb

fly

jump

swim

talk

understand

walk

want

expressions

sorry

6 Grandma's glasses

nouns

animal

armchair

child
coat
cupboard
cushion
desk
glasses
grandma
handbag
home
house
people
rug
sofa
table
toothbrush
TV
window
adjectives
black
fantastic
hot
orange
verbs
ask
drive

go
help
ride
prepositions
next to
expressions
oh dear

7 Let's go there now!
nouns
afternoon
badminton
beach
father
fishing
football
horse riding
lunchtime
morning
park
racket
sea
shell
shop
skateboard

skateboarding
sport
street
swimming
tennis
adjectives
favourite
grey
verbs
do
draw
like
live
spell

8 Not today!
nouns
apple pie
carrot
chicken
chips
clothes
donkey
egg
fish
food

fruit
garden
grape
jeans
kiwi
lemon
meatball
mice/mouse
mother
orange
sausage
shirt
shorts
snake
sweets
tomato
T-shirt
watch
adjectives
beautiful
hungry
little
verbs
drink
eat

Acknowledgements

The author would like to acknowledge the shared professionalism and FUN she's experienced whilst working with colleagues during 20 years of production of YLE tests. She would also like to thank CUP for their support in the writing of this second edition of Storyfun.

On a personal note, Karen fondly thanks her inspirational story-telling grandfather, and now, three generations later, her sons, Tom and Will, for adding so much creative fun to our continuation of the family story-telling and story-making tradition.

The author and publishers would like to thank the following ELT professionals who commented on the material at different stages of development: Idalia Luz, Portugal; Louise Manicolo, Mexico; Mark Manning, Spain; Alice Soydas, Turkey.

Design and typeset by Wild Apple Design.

Cover design and header artwork by Nicholas Jackson (Astound).

Audio production by Hart McLeod, Cambridge.

Music by Mark Fishlock and produced by Ian Harker. Recorded at The Soundhouse Studios, London.

The authors and publishers acknowledge the following sources of copyright material and are grateful for the permissions granted. While every effort has been made, it has not always been possible to identify the sources of all the material used, or to trace all copyright holders. If any omissions are brought to our notice, we will be happy to include the appropriate acknowledgements on reprinting.

The publishers are grateful to the following for permission to reproduce copyright photographs and material:

Key: BL = Below Left, BR = Below Right, CL = Centre Left, CR = Centre Right, T = Top, TC = Top Centre, TL = Top Left.

p. 68 (bike): aguirre_mar/iStock/Getty Images Plus/Getty Images; p. 68 (hat): FBP/Getty Images; p. 68 (cat): Dave King (c) Dorling Kindersley/Dorling Kindersley/Getty Images; p. 68 (doll): Luc/STOCK4B/Stock4B/Getty Images; p. 69 (B): KidStock/Blend Images/ Getty Images; p. 70 (table): colemat/iStock/Getty Images Plus/Getty Images; p. 70 (sofa): mrs_strongarm/iStock/Getty Images Plus/Getty Images; p. 70 (lamp): zzve/iStock/Getty Images Plus/Getty Images; p. 71 (park): Alistair Berg/DigitalVision/Getty Images; p. 72 (TL): KidStock/Blend Images/Getty Images; p. 72 (TR): kristian sekulic/E+/Getty Images; p. 72 (BL): goldenKB/iStock/Getty Images Plus/Getty Images; p. 72 (BR): laartist/iStock/Getty Images Plus/Getty Images; p. 73 (TL): blue jean images/Getty Images; p. 73 (TR): bo1982/E+/ Getty Images; p. 73 (BL): Wavebreakmedia Ltd/Wavebreak Media/Getty Images Plus/Getty Images; p. 73 (BR): LittleBee80/iStock/Getty Images Plus/Getty Images.

The authors and publishers are grateful to the following illustrators:

Marta Alvarez Miguens (Astound) pp. 52, 53, 54, 55, 56, 57, 58, 59; Nigel Dobbyn (Beehive) pp. 69, 71; Andy Elkerton (Sylvie Poggio) pp. 36, 37, 38, 39, 40, 41, 42, 43, 78 (banana, monkey, frog); Clive Goodyer p. 70; Kelly Kennedy (Sylvie Poggio) pp. 12, 13, 14, 15, 16, 17, 18, 19, 78 (tennis, hand, book, piano, robot, nose, doll, teddy bear); Dani Padron (Advocate) pp. 28, 29, 30, 31, 32, 33, 34, 35; Melanie Sharp (Sylvie Poggio) pp. 20, 21, 22, 23, 24, 25, 26, 27, 78 (dog, lemonade, sun); Harriet Stanes (NB Illustration) pp. 44, 45, 46, 47, 48, 49, 50, 51, 78 (bed, computer, living room); Alex Willmore (Astound) pp. 4, 5, 6, 7, 8, 9, 10, 11; Gaby Zermeño pp. 60, 61, 62, 63, 64, 65, 66, 67.